THE BASICS OF
CROSS-FUNCTIONAL TEAMS

HENRY J. LINDBORG, PH.D.

QUALITY RESOURCES.
A Division of The Kraus Organization Limited
New York, New York

Most Quality Resources books are available at quantity discounts when purchased in bulk. For more information contact:
Special Sales Department
Quality Resources
A Division of the Kraus Organization Limited
902 Broadway
New York, New York 10010
800-247-8519   212-979-8600

Copyright © 1997 Henry J. Lindborg, Ph.D.

All rights reserved. No part of this work covered by the copyrights hereon may be reproduced or used in any form or by any means—graphic, electronic, or mechanical, including photocopying, recording, taping, or information storage and retrieval systems—without written permission of the publisher.

Printed in the United States of America

01 00 99 98 97   10 9 8 7 6 5 4 3 2 1

∞

The paper used in this publication meets the minimum requirements of American National Standard for Information Sciences—Permanence of Paper for Printed Library Materials, ANSI Z39.48-1984.

ISBN 0-527-76332-2

Library of Congress Cataloging-in-Publication Data
Lindborg, Henry J.
    The basics of cross-functional teams / Henry J. Lindborg.
       p.   cm.
    Includes bibliographical references.
    ISBN 0-527-76332-2 (pb)
    1. Teams in the workplace. I. Title.
HD66.L555   1997
658.4'02—dc21   97-28136
                                                      CIP

For Mary Anne, my wife and teammate.

Contents

Preface ix

Chapter 1: Defining Cross-Functional Teams 1
　　　　　　Definition 1
　　　　　　Example: An ISO 9000 Team 3
　　　　　　Success Factors for Cross-Functional Teams .. 5
　　　　　　　　A Systems Perspective 5
　　　　　　　　Management Commitment 6
　　　　　　　　Team Development 8
　　　　　　　　How the ISO Team Example Applies ... 8
　　　　　　Basic Requirements of a Cross-Functional
　　　　　　　　Team 9
　　　　　　Summary 10

Chapter 2: Designing the Cross-Functional Team 11
　　　　　　Team Charter 11
　　　　　　Team Membership 13
　　　　　　　　Choosing a Team Leader 13
　　　　　　　　Choosing Team Members 15
　　　　　　Summary 18

Chapter 3:	Deploying Leadership Through Cross-Functional Teams 19
	Defining Leadership 20
Chapter 4:	Building Effective Cross-Functional Teams . . 23
	Supporting Cross-Functional Teams 23
	Preparing for Change. 23
	Individual and Group Values 24
	Team Values 27
	Initiating the Team 28
	Ground Rules 28
	Stages of Team Development 29
	The Inner Life of Teams 30
	Creating a Team Vision 31
	Developing Roles 32
	Team Leader 32
	Team Members 33
	Planning 33
	Managing 33
	Communicating 35
	Measuring 36
	Networking 37
	Mapping 40
	Meeting 41
	Deciding 44
	Consensus 44
	Standardized Problem-Solving 45
	Skills for Team Dialogue 47
	Managing Conflict 48
	Celebrating Team Accomplishments 51

Chapter 5: The Role of the Steering Team 53
　　　　　　The Team and Strategy 56
　　　　　　Support and Training 58
　　　　　　Customer, Supplier, and Core Process
　　　　　　　Alignment 60
　　　　　　Defining Purpose: Team Mission 62
　　　　　　Team Resources 62
　　　　　　Sponsorship 63
　　　　　　Communication 64
　　　　　　Creating the Future: Aligning for Results ... 66

Chapter 6: Conclusion 69

References 71

Further Reading 73

Preface

This small book is intended to provide an orientation for those chartering, leading, and participating in cross-functional teams. It focuses on the values that drive effective teams, and the structures required to support them. Its premise is that cross-functional teams demand a leadership perspective from everyone involved, that is, they require understanding of, and responsibility for, the goals of the organization as a whole. In fostering leadership at all levels, an organization builds a competitive edge in systems thinking and technical competence, as well as in both group and individual development.

Like other factors that provide long-term competitive advantage, cross-functional teams require planning.

Poorly implemented cross-functional teams have been frustrating and costly to companies and their employees. If cross-functional teams are properly aligned with corporate objectives, they can enhance skills in project management, contribute significantly to business results, and improve the quality of work-life. Chapter 5 provides guidance on team chartering for those involved in that process, principally managers and quality council members. The role of the steering team is placed last for two reasons: to permit the book to take a team member's perspective, which assumes chartering has taken place; and to permit team members to read about chartering with a better understanding of the nature and purposes of cross-functional teams.

Special thanks are due to Cindy Tokumitsu, editor of this volume, without whose patience and commitment to continuous improvement it would not have been completed.

CHAPTER 1

Defining Cross-Functional Teams

DEFINITION

What is the difference between a cross-functional team and other teams? What can a team member expect? These questions may arise when one is invited to participate in a cross-functional team.

Workplace teams are usually formed by management or a quality council, which charters the team to carry out a project, often involving improvement of a process. *When the project assigned to the team crosses departmental or functional boundaries, the team is a cross-functional team.* A cross-functional team is formed to achieve a common purpose and, if effective, achieves greater results than individuals working alone or departmental teams would achieve. Such a team may be formed for many purposes in very different organizations. For example: A brewer brings together key personnel from production, marketing, and advertising to develop a new beverage. An electronics firm creates a team to map processes in preparation for ISO 9000 registration. A publisher forms a strategic marketing team from a number of newspapers to explore new product opportunities. Academics from various disciplines form a team to create a new master's program in management to meet employers' needs. People with different expertise and experience are called upon to work together on a common goal outside their work group. They are challenged to become leaders and members of cross-functional teams.

Like customer focus, benchmarking, and process mapping, cross-functional teams are most often identified with quality improvement and "quality culture." They may help an organization to meet quality standards, such as ISO 9000 or QS-9000, to restructure work across departmental or functional lines, to solve problems, to offer new products or services, or to improve customer satisfaction. Sometimes these teams are intended to bring about major change, including restructuring of functional departments themselves. In other instances, the team's tasks improve processes without affecting organizational structure.

Whatever their purpose or scope, however, *cross-functional teams are always defined in relation to their organizational context; that is, they are cross-functional because they cross the boundaries of existing structures.*

A cross-functional team differs from other work groups in a number of important ways:

- The team's purpose cannot be accomplished without the involvement, perspectives, and expertise of more than one department or function.
- The team focuses on an issue or process with several "owners." More than one first-line manager or supervisor is responsible for the areas affected.
- Members come from different departments, functional areas, or disciplines.
- Team results depend upon the buy-in of persons across the organization.
- A cross-functional 91 team contributes to organizational learning. It contributes to the organization's self-understanding and future performance.

EXAMPLE: AN ISO 9000 TEAM

A team formed to help a company attain registration to one of the ISO 9000 quality standards provides a useful example. Though registration is more common among manufacturers, the ISO 9000 standards are generic and applicable to a wide variety of organizations, including service industries, education and training, consulting, and even healthcare. Developed by the International Organization for Standardization (ISO), the standards are a source of guidance in creating a basic quality system that provides assurance to customers that an organization can deliver what it promises.

The most comprehensive of the standards, ISO 9001, defines a quality assurance system for an organization that designs, develops, produces, installs, and services a product. Since our purpose is not to review the standard itself, but to see how it relates to cross-functional teams, only a few key elements will be discussed. It must be understood, however, that a company seeking registration is audited to the standard by a third party, and that preparing for the audit requires serious effort and expenditure of time and resources across the organization.

The standard describes a quality system. All of the elements of the organization that affect quality are considered. Some of these are management issues: management responsibility and authority, and allocation of resources, for example. Others, such as design control, purchasing, process control, inspection and testing, handling, delivery, and servicing, usually belong to specific departments. A significant challenge for those seeking registration is how to organize to prepare for the audit.

Usually an ISO 9000 team is formed with the mission of preparing the organization for audit. In order to ensure that all elements of the standard are accounted for, team members are chosen according to functional areas and specific expertise, such as documentation, training, and statistical methods. Members, in turn, may head teams in their own areas to ensure that requirements set forth in the standard are met.

This logical arrangement sometimes results in disaster and sometimes in success. In an electronics division of one large firm, team members obediently heard their mission, treated one another civilly, learned their parts of the standard, returned to their departments to begin deployment, and found limited cooperation among coworkers who saw little need for documentation or other requirements. In management there was little urgency or energy for registration, so as resistance mounted, ISO was quietly dropped and the team disbanded. Several years later, after a second feeble attempt, initiated and dropped by new management, an effective team was formed and registration was accomplished, against the odds.

In contrast, a manufacturer of heavy equipment formed a similar team which was resoundingly successful, readying the company for an audit within one year.

What were the differences between the failed and the successful cross-functional teams?

SUCCESS FACTORS FOR CROSS-FUNCTIONAL TEAMS

Of the many factors that can affect the success of cross-functional teams, three are critical: a systems perspective, management commitment, and team development.

A Systems Perspective

A system may be seen as an interacting, interdependent group of elements or objects that together create a uniform whole. The parts are different but interdependent. The human body, a school, a health care organization, a nuclear plant may all be seen in terms of systems.

In order to plan for personal or organizational change, we need to see how parts of a system relate to the whole. The successful ISO team began not only with instructions on what needed to be done, but with an understanding of how each of their departments contributed to the quality system (see Figure 1.1).

The team also developed an understanding of the relationships among departments in meeting customer expectations. As we grow in understanding systems, we move from seeing objects as unrelated, to seeing them within organizational structures, to discovering relationships among elements (see Figure 1.2).

```
┌─────────────────────────────────────────────────────────┐
│   QUALITY COUNCIL              SALES                    │
│   * Internal Audits            * Contract Review        │
│                                * Servicing              │
│                                                         │
│   QUALITY                                               │
│   * Receiving Inspection & Test                         │
│   * In-Process Inspection & Test    ENGINEERING         │
│   * Final Inspection & Test      Quality   * Design & Dev. Planning │
│   * Inspection & Test Records    System    * Design Output          │
│   * Inspection, M&TE                        * Design Verification    │
│   * Inspection & Test Status                * Design Changes         │
│   * Control of Nonconformities                          │
│   * Corrective Action                                   │
│                                                         │
│   HUMAN RESOURCES          EXECUTIVE MANAGEMENT         │
│   * Training               * Management Review          │
│                                                         │
│                      OPERATIONS                         │
│   Purchasing:        Manufacturing Engineering:  Material Management: │
│   * Assessment of Sub-Contractors  * Documented Work Instructions  * Handling │
│   * Purchasing Data                * Approval of Processes & Equipment  * Storage │
│   * Verification of Purchased Product  * Special Processes  * Packaging │
│   * Purchaser Supplied Product                           * Delivery │
│   * Product I.D. & Traceability                         │
└─────────────────────────────────────────────────────────┘
```

Figure 1.1. Parts of system as they relate to the whole.
Diagram courtesy of Richard Justus.

Because the successful team saw the big picture, members were able to communicate the meaning of the standard in terms of a common goal: meeting customer requirements. They were also able to show their own departments where they fit.

A systems perspective by itself, however, does not guarantee success.

Management Commitment

A second success factor was management commitment. A team culture needs to be leadership-driven and supported by project management skills.

Defining Cross-Functional Teams 7

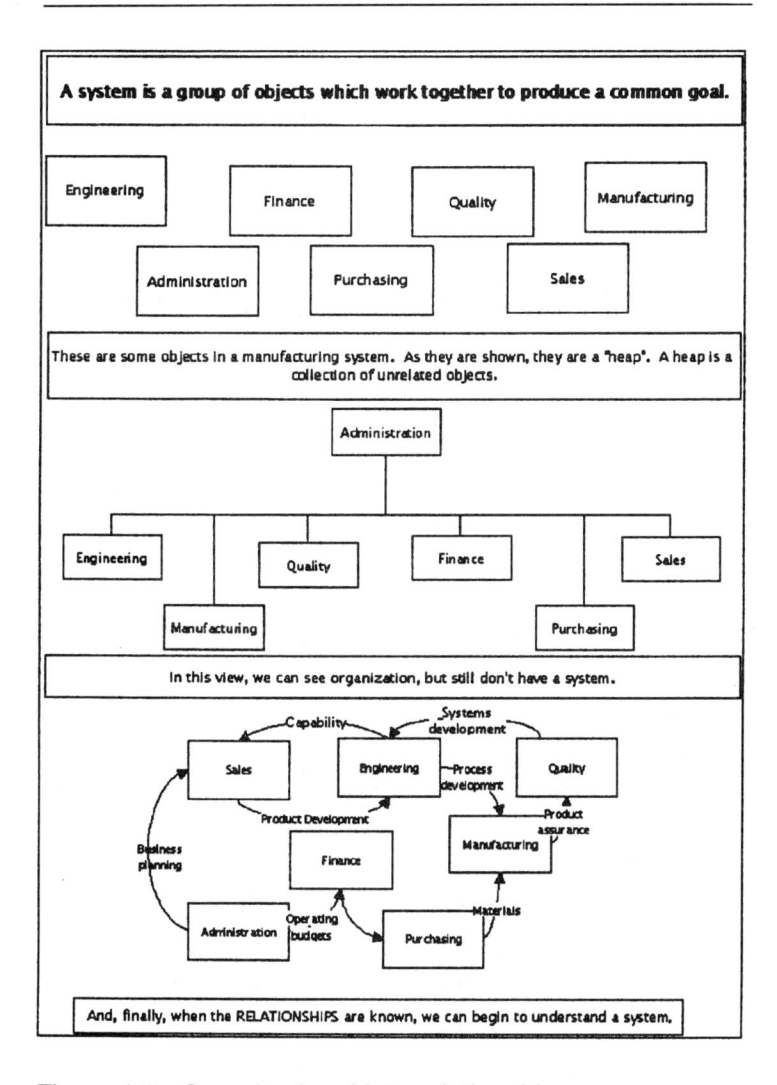

A system is a group of objects which work together to produce a common goal.

Engineering Finance Quality Manufacturing

Administration Purchasing Sales

These are some objects in a manufacturing system. As they are shown, they are a "heap". A heap is a collection of unrelated objects.

```
                    Administration
          ┌────────┬────────┬────────┐
    Engineering  Quality  Finance  Sales
       Manufacturing        Purchasing
```

In this view, we can see organization, but still don't have a system.

[Diagram showing relationships: Capability, Systems development, Process development, Product Development, Product assurance, Business planning, Operating budgets, Materials — connecting Sales, Engineering, Quality, Finance, Manufacturing, Administration, Purchasing]

And, finally, when the RELATIONSHIPS are known, we can begin to understand a system.

Figure 1.2. Organizational interrelationships.

Diagram courtesy of John Zavacki.

At the electronics firm, management was unconvinced of the quality system's real value and pursued registration only to emulate other divisions of the corporation. The manufacturer was sure that registration would provide competitive advantage. There, management communicated the importance of a customer assurance system, provided education on how each department had its part to play, and supported the ISO team at every stage of its work with resources and encouragement.

Team Development

A third success factor was team development. The manufacturer knew not only how to structure teams, but how to organize teams, provide them a framework for their own decision-making, and keep them motivated by understanding and communicating the value of their contributions. Once management of the electronics firm took the ISO challenge seriously, communicated effectively, and provided resources for team development, success was possible.

How the ISO Team Example Applies

How is this ISO example important for thinking about cross-functional teams? For one thing, quality systems have been a "proving ground" for such teams. Because cross-functional teams are vital in establishing and maintaining effective quality systems, the automotive industry's QS-9000 standard explicitly requires their formation. For another, the example meets the criteria for defining a cross-functional team, and may help in predicting what may be encountered in any such team.

First, ISO registration could not be accomplished without management commitment to attain a strategic objective that crossed functional boundaries and involved persons from each function.

Second, in order to achieve its mission, the ISO team had to address a quality system, not only its parts. Members were chosen according to how their areas contributed to the system. The "big picture" was necessary to communicate the importance of the team's work to the organization as a whole and within departments. Without it, employees could not relate new requirements on how to coordinate and document their work to any overarching purpose.

Third, team members played several roles: they contributed to installation of the whole system; provided expertise from their own department or discipline; and provided communication, and in some instances, team leadership, within their departments.

Finally, the team contributed to organizational improvement and learning. The quality system it deployed is regularly audited and maintained with feedback loops for ongoing corrective action.

BASIC REQUIREMENTS OF A CROSS-FUNCTIONAL TEAM

Members of the manufacturer's ISO team found the basic requirement of a cross-functional team in place: A mission or purpose had been defined for the team. In this case, the mission of preparing the organization for audit came from management, which identified a sponsor of the project at the vice-presidential level. Resources for the team were allocated and a team leader—who would manage the project, keep records, delegate tasks, and conduct meetings—was appointed.

The company provided the team with a facilitator who understood quality systems, quality decision-making tools, and group interaction. This facilitator offered suggestions on how to keep meeting records, including a simple PC-based system for use by the appointed "recorder" or "scribe."

At the first meeting, the team leader presented a charter, including a statement of what the team was to accomplish (its mission), why this needed to be accomplished (history), what the team could do (the scope and limitation of its authority), the team's resources (expressed in dollars, human resources, time), and a suggested time line. The charter was accompanied by maps of the core processes affected by the project and the customers and suppliers involved.

The team members were expected to understand the mission, participate in meetings, carry out assigned tasks, and represent a functional area. In this case, team members also functioned as team leaders within their areas. Members' responsibilities therefore mirrored those of the ISO team leader, and required some team leader training.

SUMMARY

In summary, this cross-functional team differs from one that might be set up within a department or work group in several important ways. First, it requires a systems perspective since its mission encompasses all of the company's activities affecting quality. Second, it requires that members play a dual role, contributing expertise in their areas, while interacting with others from different backgrounds in attaining a corporate objective. Finally, members must buy in to the team's goals within their functional areas. Though most cross-functional teams don't require members to lead other teams, they usually do require members to interface with both their own areas and with other functions in the organization.

What follows are some basics for working in such cross-functional teams. They include designing teams, establishing the roles of team leaders and team members, as well as providing organizational support needed to build effective teams.

CHAPTER 2
Designing the Cross-Functional Team

TEAM CHARTER

Companies produce good track records when they provide teams with clear goals consistent with corporate objectives and the resources, including time and expertise, to attain them. We often call this "empowerment," the ability to exercise competence and judgment within a framework of authority.

A major Wisconsin food company provides a good illustration of how successful teams are developed. At this plant, where team participation is strictly voluntary, involvement approaches 90%. Employees may be involved in four types of teams: action teams composed of those performing similar work; ad hoc project teams; teams formed as the result of an employee action request; and cross-functional continuous improvement teams focused on a product or a manufacturing process. In each instance, management is directly involved and overall guidance comes from a Quality Steering Committee. Direct management involvement, explicit values, and criteria for formation keep teams on track.

The clarity and completeness of a team's charter (the document authorizing the team and providing guidance in its formation) are good predictors of a team's success. An effective charter helps avoid common pitfalls of cross-functional teams:

- lack of management support
- absence of clear goals
- failure to develop performance measures
- failure to manage projects and keep time lines

In specifying resources, including a sponsor (a higher level manager who will foster the work of the team), the charter defines management support. In defining a mission, it sets the team on track.

A good chartering process (covered in detail in Chapter 5) provides a new cross-functional team with a well-developed mission and the resources to carry it out. A mission is simply a statement of what the team is to do—the problem it is to solve, the process it is to improve, or the product it is to develop.

Because the team crosses boundaries of existing departments or functions and requires a systems perspective, it is important that team members are told not only *what* to do but *why they are to do it.* Effective chartering therefore includes background information on how the team's mission is related to corporate objectives and how the organization will be improved once the mission is complete. In other words, the team is presented with a "gap analysis" that shows the present state and the desired outcome.

A gap analysis helps the team build support for the project inside the organization and serves as a basis for developing performance measures. By stating how the organization will be different if the team completes its work, the charter offers a goal to which members can commit. It also provides guidance in the kinds of measures the team can best employ. By specifying if the gap is in production (quantity), meeting customer needs (quality), cost, timeliness, quality of work life (human factors), or other areas, the charter can help the team decide if it can apply a numeric measure or percentage, or describe how its performance will meet customer expectations, the customer being the manager or quality body that has chartered the team. For example, a hospital's safety team was able to identify a measure in the number of occurrences of a particular kind of accident. On the other hand, the ISO team, with the mission of preparing the organization for a successful audit to the ISO 9001 standard, chose its measures by examining the objectives of each step in the project plan. In both instances, measures were developed from the charter.

Finally, the team should have a clear understanding of available resources. These resources include time, money, and expertise. Time is a critical resource, and an estimated time line for the completion of the team's work ought to be part of a charter.

TEAM MEMBERSHIP

Choosing a Team Leader

Though high-performing teams demonstrate a spirit of equality, leaders play an important role in keeping teams on track.

Under ordinary circumstances, the team leader is appointed by management or a quality council rather than elected by the team. Appointment confers management approval for the leader to network across the organization. The leader's role is to bring together a diverse and sometimes skeptical group for a common purpose, ensure effective team processes, and manage a team project that crosses functional boundaries. A team leader should understand the impact of change, support meaningful change aligned with organizational objectives, help create an environment for learning, and employ tools and techniques that will provide direction and measure progress for team-based decision-making.

Criteria for appointment of a team leader should include:

- A stake in the team's mission. The leader should identify with the team's objectives. If, for example, the development of a new soft drink involves production, marketing, and sales, the marketing representative who had encouraged new product development may be a logical choice.

- Technical competence. The leader should be recognized as good at whatever she or he does. This inspires trust during team formation. If a marketer is known to have developed effective campaigns for well-known brands, he or she may have more initial credibility with the new team—even if team leadership is a new role.

- Interpersonal skills. The leader should have knowledge of communication systems, team formation, decision-making, and conflict resolution. He or she should have a track record of inspiring trust and cooperation.

- Project management skills. The leader should know how to deploy resources, organize work, and focus on outcomes.

- Adaptability and flexibility. The leader should recognize change as opportunity, and be able to modify plans to meet changes in the work environment.

- A spirit of service. The leader should want to make this contribution.

The appointed leader should begin to work with the team's sponsor and/or the chartering body to obtain information and review customer expectations. Since the primary customer of the team is the chartering body, these expectations should be reviewed, refined, and if necessary, documented. The leader also does a preliminary review of customers and stakeholders affected by the project, examines processes involved, and evaluates proposed resources.

The chartering body should support the leader in the selection of team members and negotiation for time.

Choosing Team Members

Team members are often chosen by managers. For cross-functional teams, I recommend giving the leader the authority to choose members in consultation with specific managers. The team leader can use the charter to communicate with a manager, show how his or her area is involved in the project, and obtain advice on whose expertise the team requires most.

Care should be taken to make sure that the team is complete. A newspaper team, whose mission was to improve an entertainment section, included representatives from editorial, production, and distribution. The team had been formed in response to a reader survey that evaluated the product. The team decided to integrate national entertainment news with local arts events. After a few months, however, the team was reconvened because of minimal advertising support. This time, the team called upon the sales department who surveyed advertisers and found them reluctant to place ads in a section with a "tabloid" format. The section's design was changed, more ads were placed, production costs were reduced, and increased revenue resulted. If the first team had included people from sales, it might have avoided unnecessary rework and loss of revenue during the quarter.

While organizations sometimes use a variety of psychological and group dynamics instruments (personality assessments) for team formation, the cross-functional team leader will probably be guided by the need for representation and expertise from affected departments or functions. At the same time, the leader has to look for—or be ready to help develop—team skills in potential members. Since a systems orientation is required, these skills go beyond technical competence and social skills.

As team members participate with diverse colleagues in examining systems, they will maintain their own roles within their departments or functions. For many team members this produces tension brought on by additional responsibilities in unfamiliar areas, as well as conflicting values. As an individual member in a department, they "own" their areas of competence and control. They understand their accountability, value their working relationships with peers, and are able to evaluate their own performance. As a member of a cross-functional team, they are called to mutual accountability with a new, and perhaps unfamiliar, group. They must work independently and interdependently as they evaluate themselves and others in new roles and critique systems.

In addition to technical competence, members should be selected based on interpersonal skills, analytical and problem-solving abilities, skills in developing new ideas and possible alternatives, and systems capabilities. These may be developed through training and experience in disciplined teams. Organizations that want to design new cross-functional teams should encourage team leaders and managers to begin developing criteria for team selection that will become part of the quality management system. As organizations become more team-based, criteria for team membership, as well as for employment, will include team participation skills. This scenario was illustrated in a 1992 report identifying orientations and skills that employers look for (see Table 2.1). Interestingly, these closely parallel attributes team leaders look for in members.

Table 2.1. Employers' Needs

Orientation	Definition
Customer orientation	Customer needs and our solutions to their problems are why organizations exist; all employees must continually strive to improve customer satisfaction
Practical knowledge and application of Total Quality tools	Hands-on skill in using Total Quality processes and tools
Fact-based decision making	The need for the right data at the right time for the right action; "What do I need to know?" and "How will I act on that information?"
Understanding that work is a process	Work is a process organized around outcomes; as a process, work can be improved and refined—even radically overhauled—to achieve improvement
Team orientation	Ability to work effectively with others; minimize unproductive conflict while encouraging diverse opinions and constructive debate; valuing the greater good of the company above personal, unit, or functional goals
Commitment to improvement	Continuously striving for improvement, from the small and incremental to the big breakthroughs
Active learner	Learning is central to success; ability to gain insight by reflecting on successes and failures; to learn from coworkers, competitors, and customers
Systems perspective	Ability to see "the big picture," across hierarchical, organizational, and functional boundaries

Source: Employers' Needs Working Council (1992).

SUMMARY

In designing cross-functional teams, team chartering and recruiting are key areas. The team charter must include the following critical elements:

- well-developed mission statement
- background information
- resources available

In recruiting for team membership, the team leader should be appointed and given the authority to recruit team members. Team members should be selected based on area of expertise and team skills.

CHAPTER 3

Deploying Leadership Through Cross-Functional Teams

Successful cross-functional teams affect an organization in two important ways: First, they bring about improvements that cannot be accomplished by departments or functions working alone. Second, they change the "world-view" of the organization and of individual team members, moving them to greater interdependence. For cross-functional teams to be valuable in the long run, they require practical, common-sense development of systems, core values, and skill sets.

Certain requirements are necessary in developing teams. Among them are team values, defined systems, and team skills. Team values are critical to motivate behavior and establish performance criteria. Defined systems enable us to work together effectively and help define projects with strategic importance. They help us see work as a process and understand how things fit together. With systems skills we can align our values with our outcomes. If we have good interpersonal and facilitation skills, we can create bonds and make good decisions. Skills can be learned and enhanced.

In conducting training for cross-functional teams, I have asked team members to define what they do as teams evolve. The behaviors described by team members fell into categories closely resembling those describing the behavior of leaders. This should not be surprising, since both organizational leaders and cross-functional teams have a systems perspective and must seek cooperation at every level of the organization. Detecting leadership behavior in cross-functional teams suggests that the futurist rhetoric that leadership skills will be required of all of us has some foundation, especially in organizations that increasingly structure themselves around projects managed by teams.

DEFINING LEADERSHIP

Overall, effective cross-functional teams are exercises in successful leadership. They depend upon skilled leaders for guidance, but as groups they take collective responsibility to behave like leaders. Successful leaders of cross-functional teams ensure that the *team as a whole and its individual members systematically perform important leadership behaviors* for both effective project management and creation of team spirit.

Using categories developed by Gary Yuckl, 15 leadership behaviors can be identified and related to team performance (Table 3.1).

Table 3.1. Leadership Behaviors Related to Team Performance

Behavior	Team Performance
Supporting	A climate of trust established. Differences recognized and affirmed. Workload adjusted.
Consulting	Team leader provides direction while building consensus. Standards for meeting management are established.
Delegating	Team members assigned roles and responsibilities.
Recognizing	Individual efforts are appreciated and "celebrated."
Rewarding	Reward system includes team participation. The team's performance is evaluated.
Motivating	Team purpose is meaningful to each member.
Managing Conflict	Conflicting viewpoints encouraged while interpersonal harmony and "spirit" are maintained.
Developing	Individuals are mentored. They understand how team participation enhances individual and professional growth. Team skills are defined, learned, and practiced.
Clarifying	Goals are specified. Scope of the team's mission is clearly defined and documented. Stakeholders and affected processes are identified.
Planning and Organizing	Team's activities are documented in a project plan that includes time, resources, quality standards, and risk management.
Problem-Solving	Problem-solving and consensus building techniques are agreed upon.
Informing	Communication plan established, specifying how information will be disseminated among team members and to stakeholders.
Monitoring	Activities are defined and sequenced. Milestones are established.
Representing	The team mission is internalized by team members. They identify with the team project and communicate its purpose.
Networking and Interfacing	The team leader and team members understand organizational culture and dynamics. They create relationships that facilitate the work of the team with resources and information.

The processes through which teams are built and developed, covered in Chapters 4 and 5, provide the basis for the development of the leadership behaviors that successful teams exhibit.

CHAPTER 4
Building Effective Cross-Functional Teams

SUPPORTING CROSS-FUNCTIONAL TEAMS

Preparing for Change

Where cross-functional teams are new, they represent change. When well implemented, they bring about change, and change creates stress. In organizations seeking to compete in a difficult environment, employees may see change as imperiling their ability to make a living for themselves or their families. For example, total quality management may attack a source of self-esteem in their personal ownership of management responsibility by assigning it to a team. Corporate traditions and a sense of belonging may be undermined by new structures and ways of interacting with others. To provide support for members in reaching common goals, cross-functional teams need to build a climate of trust while planning change.

Planned change is a transition from our present state (where we are) to our desired state (where we want to be). The transition is marked by a number of disturbing manifestations:

- Low stability
- High emotional stress
- High, often undirected energy
- Control becomes an issue
- Past behavior patterns are valued
- Conflict increases.

In teams, for example, ambiguity about order and control undermines consensus decision-making. Members may find themselves less willing to risk exposing how they think and feel. During change, team members may want to return to older ways of doing things. The role of the team leader becomes critical in providing support that will reduce confusion while fostering participation by persons who interpret their work lives differently from one another.

Individual and Group Values

Cross-functional teams bring together people with differing perspectives and knowledge to achieve the best possible results. In values terms, cross-functional teams rely on diversity and interdependence. Stephen Covey has identified interdependence as important to individual and corporate effectiveness. Procter and Gamble found the value of diversity so powerful that the corporation made it a criterion in team formation, requiring that persons with different outlooks and discipline backgrounds be included in teams.

Cross-functional teams are by nature diverse, but they have to work at valuing diversity and creating interdependence.

Team leaders need to confront not only the possibility of "turf wars" by departments, but real differences in world-view among members. A world-view is how an individual or an organization sees reality. It is the combination of the values that motivate us as individuals or groups. We are most aware of our own world-view when we encounter those who don't share it. For example, a manager who values hierarchy, propriety, and order may find it hard to deal with a "think tank" of young computer systems designers who practice equality, informality, and creativity.

> A World-View is an overall perspective on life which encompasses the way a person perceives the world, evaluates and responds to it.
> (Rudolf A. Makkreel)

Our values are most reinforced by our work groups. In work groups we interpret reality together and create norms about "how things should be." We sometimes call these norms an "organizational culture," though in many organizations there are a number of "cultures." A newspaper, for example, requires a sales force, editorial staff, reporters, layout, production, and delivery personnel. These groups embrace a wide range of different professional values: individual achievement and economic success, craftsmanship and art, efficiency and planning, productivity, free speech, and community welfare. While each group may have a good "team spirit" and high professional competence, there is no guarantee they see things alike, in spite of a corporate mission statement and their mutual desire that the paper succeed. Here are several examples:

- An effort to improve press and delivery times was stalled by differing cultures and department-based interpretation of deadlines in a team composed of customer service, editorial, pressroom, and delivery personnel. Similar differences in culture and understanding of processes in a team of college faculty, staff, and administration attempting to improve student advisement led to frustration and abandonment of the effort.

- In a manufacturing organization, new product development depends upon cooperation among research and development, production, marketing, and financial departments. A highly specialized metal fabricator found that while its revenues depended upon innovation, its effective design and development work was undermined by failure to attend to marketing and management skills. The company was at risk because innovation was not a corporate-wide value. Production responded slowly, and financial officers were reluctant to invest in new, specialized equipment. Only a fiscal crisis brought these functions together to examine their assumptions and commit to innovation.
- A study of nursing personnel found that those with the same job descriptions had similar values. Values of care were found across groups, but administrators valued creating new organizational forms more highly.
- Another study identified an engineering culture that focuses on technology and tries to design human beings out of the picture. In a values study of a college, strong motivation to make decisions was found among board and administration, but was less a driver for faculty and staff.

Such differences occur within almost all cross-functional teams, and their effects are not always easy to predict. Nurses may need to focus on common ground in looking for new ways to better serve patients. College teams may spend time recognizing that not everyone relates to "empowerment" in the same way, and customer service teams including engineers should respect different professional orientations to work.

New members of a cross-functional teams should assess their own values. They should ask, "Of what in my work life am I most proud?" The answer is probably a good index to values. If members are willing to share their answers to this question, they often find that the things they most value may be quite different from those valued by others. This exercise helps members to explore their differences in a positive light.

Team Values

An organization can best support teams by establishing norms and procedures that keep members focused on a common goal while they learn from diversity. Team leaders and members need to work at what Barry Heermann, director of the Expanded Learning Institute in Dayton, Ohio, calls "spirit, the essence of team." It is the deep personal connection we feel with others when engaged in meaningful work and is closely related to trust.

In effective cross-functional teams there is a high level of trust. The team performs well because the leader and members consistently display competence, support, and integrity. Trust is not to be confused with simple cooperation. We can cooperate with those we don't trust (as many international treaties show us). A team should go beyond cooperation to willingness to take risks. In a cross-functional team, this risk involves professional identity. Many team members identify trust with their own professional roles. Within their fields they are trusted (and trust others) because they are competent and consistently meet performance expectations. When they join a cross-functional team, they may be working with a group of strangers outside of their fields. It is therefore important that each member is affirmed for his or her own competence. During formation, the leader should provide information on each member's responsibilities, and the first team meeting should include time for communicating what each member brings to the team, both professionally and personally. Members should be prepared to make disclosures about themselves that they are comfortable sharing.

Team results depend upon the balance of the professional and personal contribution each member makes. In order to develop interdependence, the team needs to recognize and respect the role each member plays in the organization and on the team, as well as that each role is played by a human being. Persons who embrace values of hierarchy and obedience may deal with others primarily in terms of their formal roles. Others, who incline toward individualism, may focus on the person at the expense of structures and accountability. Both require development of skills to become interdependent, valuing both formal roles and personal contribution.

Affirming members' professional competence provides a foundation of trust for cross-functional teams. Participants understand that their skills are recognized and appreciated as a contribution. At the same time, the team needs to create an atmosphere that supports development of competence in team skills. In order to inspire trust based on mutual support and integrity, the team should establish ground rules and develop them throughout its life.

INITIATING THE TEAM

Ground Rules

At the outset, the team leader should initiate discussion of rules of conduct. Sometimes the corporation will have established these through team training that covers rules for participation and problem-solving. Whether they come from a team manual or not, however, ground rules need to be agreed upon, documented, and regularly reviewed throughout the life of the team. As the team develops, the rules will be seen from new perspectives and modified. Members should be encouraged to speak up if they think an important issue is being omitted. Ground rules are the "glue" that keeps teams together.

Stages of Team Development

Many team members want some guidance on how to predict the course of team development. There are some generalizations that may be helpful. Descriptions of stages of team development have generally followed the forming, storming, norming, and performing model. That is, a team is formed. Members explore their task and get to know one another. They experience conflict and respond emotionally. Greater unity is established as roles are defined, and the team produces results. In practice these stages are not very neat, and teams sometimes revert to earlier stages, looping back to conflict and establishing new norms. There is, however, solid evidence that at about the midway point in the life of teams, they experience significant turmoil, reexamine their task and their values, and emerge with new focus as they move toward completion.

Another pattern to help orient members to what happens during the life of a team identifies five phases of a team's life: initiating, where belonging is established; visioning, where a desired state is clearly seen; claiming, where members "buy in" in a practical and personal way; celebrating, where achievement is recognized and contributions acknowledged; and letting go, where members engage in constructive feedback that frees them from obstacles to service. These phases are presented in the image of a spiral rather than a line. As teams develop, they revisit phases at new levels. For example, at the mid-point of its life, a team may well renew its vision and reclaim roles according to what it has learned by "letting go" of feelings or behaviors that have blocked its path to success.

THE INNER LIFE OF TEAMS

Service
: In performing service, teams value and honor those they serve, and the team delivers service that both surprises and delights.

Initiating
: Team members come together, to establish and re-establish their relationships and their direction, creating belonging and a sense of trust.

Visioning
: Team members create a compelling shared image of customer satisfaction that inspires work.

Claiming
: Team members empower themselves by claiming the goals, roles, competence and resources necessary to realize their vision.

Celebrating
: Team members acknowledge what their work as a team has accomplished.

Letting Go
: Team members communicate their disappointments, their frustrations and their withheld thoughts, doing so in a manner that is forthright, disclosing and with constructive feedback.

Source: Barry Heermann, *Building Team Spirit: Activities for Inspiring and Energizing Teams,* McGraw-Hill, Inc., 1997. Used with permission of the author.

CREATING A TEAM VISION

If the chartering process is effective, the team is presented with a clear statement of what it needs to do. However, in order to own the mission, the team needs to create a vision. The word "vision" often calls to mind something hazy and grandiose, not practical. And some visions fit that description. Here vision means an appreciation of the difference the project will make. A simple technique for providing a team vision is to have each team member take 10 or 15 minutes to write a newsletter article, with the project's completion date, describing the changes the team has brought about. Often members embellish these, and they serve as a good "icebreaker." But the exercise is intended to put members in the future, to have them see (vision) the meaning of what they are to accomplish. After sharing individual visions, members can identify vision elements or themes and write a common statement. The team's vision should also include the customers and stakeholders affected by the project. Simply listing these gives members a better sense of the project's impact and provides an initial understanding of process owners and others with whom communication will be required.

Until the team visions the project and understands the contribution it will make, it is unlikely that members will be motivated. Because work across departments, functions, and disciplines is often demanding and complex, a clear vision provides energy for team initiation and along the way, as problems are identified.

A consumer products manufacturer found that a team program was meeting with resistance. The work of teams was being done by a few members, whose areas were most affected. Employees were unwilling to volunteer for teams, and repeated consultation with a team training firm proved futile.

When they met, teams followed the rules but accomplished little. Why? Their work was not meaningful to the group. It could be accomplished by a few persons working alone. A good test of a team project is whether it engenders shared vision. If it doesn't, maybe it's not appropriate for a cross-functional team.

DEVELOPING ROLES

Like other teams, the cross-functional team needs a leader, a recorder, and a facilitator to advise on and monitor group processes. Team members must participate in decision-making and carry out assignments designated in the overall project plan and at meetings. Beyond these, however, are other roles. The sponsor of the cross-functional team—the senior manager who provides ongoing support—takes on an important mentoring role and should be prepared to help the team leader in communicating the team's vision across functional lines.

Team Leader

As the work of the team progresses, the leader may find additional resources are required. Both the sponsor's influence and the leader's skills will be important in calling upon the advice and expertise of others. The leader will also need to balance the roles of project manager, getting the work done, and coach, bringing out the best in each team member. As project manager, the leader calls members to their responsibilities. As coach, he or she calls them to their potential. In cross-functional teams this can be a challenge because achievement outside of a member's work group is sometimes seen as having no payoff. The leader is also a mentor, and should help each member define how they can benefit professionally from work on the team and provide assignments that permit individual development.

Team Members

Team members are accountable to the leader for carrying out all of the tasks assigned to them during the project. These may be accomplished long-term or between meetings. For major areas of delegation, the leader and member should review the member's competencies and skills, resources available, time lines, and how the member will network in the organization. Each significant delegation should be planned as a small project. For example, a team member assigned to collect data on customer satisfaction at a newspaper had to interface with four departments and review a number of surveys. By applying principles of project management, she and the team leader were able to obtain the time and resources she required.

PLANNING

Planning consists of several major components: managing, communicating, measuring, networking, and mapping.

Managing

To keep work on track, the team should create a project plan, including all of the activities and resources required to complete its mission. After defining the requirements of the project, the team should specify the activities required for completion, sequence these activities, estimate their duration, and develop a schedule adjusted to realistic time constraints. The plan should be understandable to members, as well as to those with whom the team must communicate. Critical tasks should be clear, detailed, and specifically related to resources required.

A useful tool for the team will be the Gantt chart, a horizontal bar chart that displays the time relationships among pro-

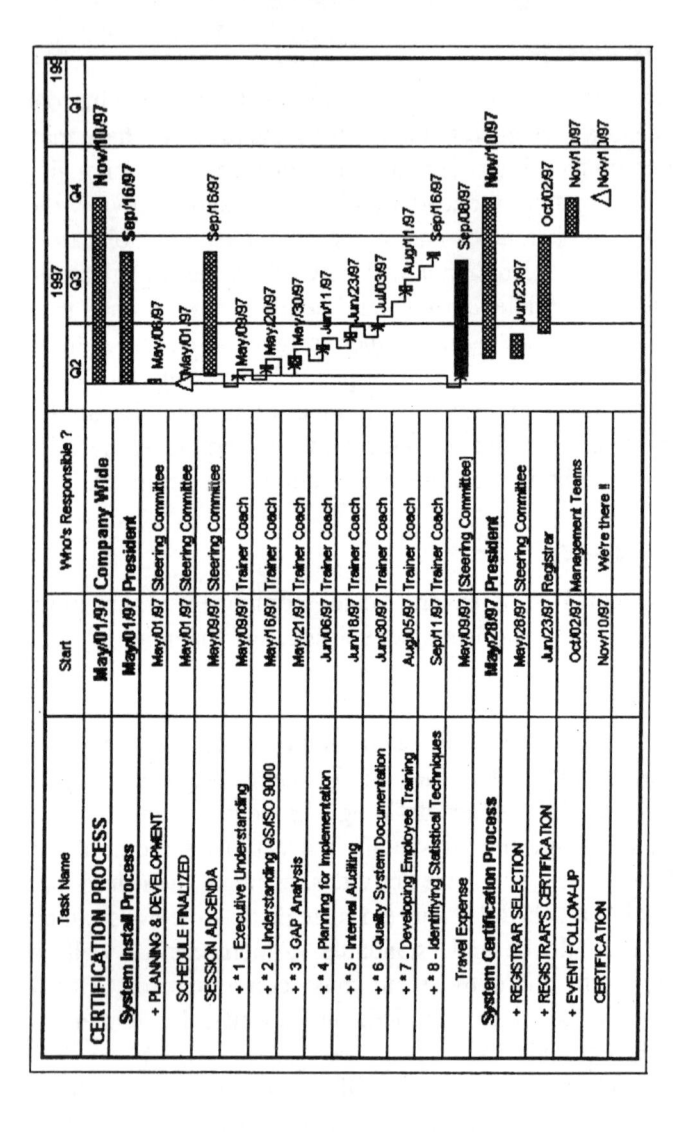

Figure 4.1. Gantt chart describing relationships among project tasks.

ject tasks (see Figure 4.1). For most team projects, a simple Gantt chart, developed from a list of necessary activities, will be a helpful first step in providing a visual representation of the team's plan.

Computer programs for project management are readily available. This software often includes means to track costs as well as activities. For more complex projects, training in PERT (Program Evaluation and Review Technique) or Critical Path Method (CPM) may be required.

Whatever technique or technology is employed, the team should identify significant milestones in its progress, points at which important activities are to be or have been completed. The duration of each activity should be estimated and monitored, as should costs. Milestones are important for communication with sponsors, customers, and stakeholders. A documented plan is important because it provides for cost and time management, becomes a means of monitoring progress, and clarifies delegation of tasks. For ease of communication, whenever possible, simple visual representation of the project should be used to keep the big picture in focus.

Communicating

Team communication should be based upon a plan that addresses the following: Who needs information. When they need it. In what form will it be communicated. Meeting minutes and reports should be made available in a timely manner, posted in hard copy, on intranet, or by e-mail. Reports on the status of the project are of particular interest to the chartering body and sponsors. The needs of all of those affected by the project should be considered in planning communication. Early communication is especially important with those whose assistance will be required later in the project. Likewise, it is important for team members to communicate with all of those affected as they carry out independently work delegated by the leader. At the outset the team should determine where information it collects will be housed, how it will be disseminated, and how it will be disposed of when the project ends.

Measuring

As part of its planning, the team ought to agree upon performance measures. The team itself needs to assess progress at each stage, measure its performance in meetings, and evaluate its overall effectiveness in task and personal achievements. Measures are developed from the team's charter (What are requirements of the "desired state"?), team dynamics (How did we perform together?), individual performance (What did I contribute?), and task completion (How did we meet the objectives of our plan?).

A simple technique for developing measures is to have the team first define a few "critical success factors" for each kind of performance. These are the areas in which the team or individual needs to be successful to bring about high performance. For each factor the team identifies measures. For example, a new hospital team made up of a board member, physicians, administrators, and clinical support, identified full participation as a critical success factor for team dynamics. They decided on a few simple measures of participation, for example, meeting attendance and response to communications, and carefully tracked them as decision-making proceeded. Performance was enhanced by agreed-upon measures. Another team in a computer company experienced delays in completing their project. Identifying critical success factors and measures for project management, such as the actual time required to complete tasks, helped revitalize the team.

Networking

Awareness of the organization's world-view will assist the team in planning how best to network as it seeks support, information, and resources for its work and develops an understanding of its own dynamics. A few simple models of how the organization thinks about planning can be helpful to the team in identifying corporate culture and setting strategies. In reviewing key questions about each of these models, the team can uncover assumptions about how it understands the organization.

- Command and Control
  Do we depend upon following orders?

This world-view is sometimes created by founders, and is usually based upon personal expertise and past success. It may also be the mode of management under increased stress and assumes that plans are handed down to and carried out by subordinates. It is sometimes found as "a present state" in organizations that aspire to "quality transformation."

Command and control can suggest an organization that is authoritarian or familial, with strong survival and territorial values embraced by managers. In this environment, the role, power, and influence of the sponsor and team leader are critical.

- Shared Values
  Do we depend upon implicit understandings and shared values?

This approach is found in a variety of entrepreneurial, religious, and non-profit organizations. In a start-up company founded by like-minded entrepreneurs, shared values and flexible organizational development substitute for control systems.

Religious and charitable organizations, though they can have long histories and established hierarchies, may also work on the basis of shared values, often derived from the mission of the founder. College and university faculties frequently operate in this mode.

Shared values become critical when institutions merge. For example, cross-functional teams effecting mergers between hospitals and regional clinics often surface differences in values taken for granted in each institution.

Teams in an environment of shared values require special attention, especially in developing techniques for surfacing assumptions and managing change. In this environment, teams need to be sure that they have top management support for change and that they communicate in terms of the organization's core mission.

- Rational Planning
  Do we depend upon a rational, predictive view of reality?

Rational planning is built on the assumption that with enough data a predictive model can be designed. Data are collected and plans are formulated by departments dedicated to that task. Management deploys the plans to be carried out by employees. This approach differs from command and control in its reliance on data gathering and the work of professional planners. Organizations embracing rational planning tend to be hierarchical and dedicated to rationality, sometimes to the exclusion of creativity and intuition. For example, a cross-functional process improvement team at a computer company was able to quickly produce sophisticated decision matrices, but failed to confront interpersonal conflict between department managers. The team's recommendations never had full effect because of failure to confront the "messy" human side of quality.

Teams in a rational environment will probably enjoy the benefits of clear direction and project management and measurement orientations. However, they may not be encouraged to explore the "spirit" of teams or to embrace the "softer" quality disciplines. To gain support and resources, teams need to provide clear communication, backed by data.

- Shared Strategy
Do we depend upon participation?

A shared strategy is developed through scanning and anticipating the needs of internal and external customers. It is developed employing many of the same technologies of rational planning but puts greater emphasis on partnerships and participation, with ongoing feedback loops. Corporations such as Xerox, Procter and Gamble, and Motorola are able to coordinate and communicate their strategies in ways that permit each employee to understand his or her part in meeting corporate objectives. The ideal structure of this approach is embodied in the Malcolm Baldrige National Quality Award.

Teams in an environment of shared strategy will often deal with strategic issues. They require a high degree of ongoing training, development, and sophistication in linking quality improvement with business results. In this environment, affected stakeholders will expect to have information and input.

- Evolving Strategy
Do we depend upon creativity?

An evolving strategy is found in organizations that are highly creative and seek breakthrough products and services. This orientation to strategy is sometimes found in "skunk works" that run parallel to corporate divisions. Evolving strategy depends upon fostering good ideas that emerge from research and development or brainstorming.

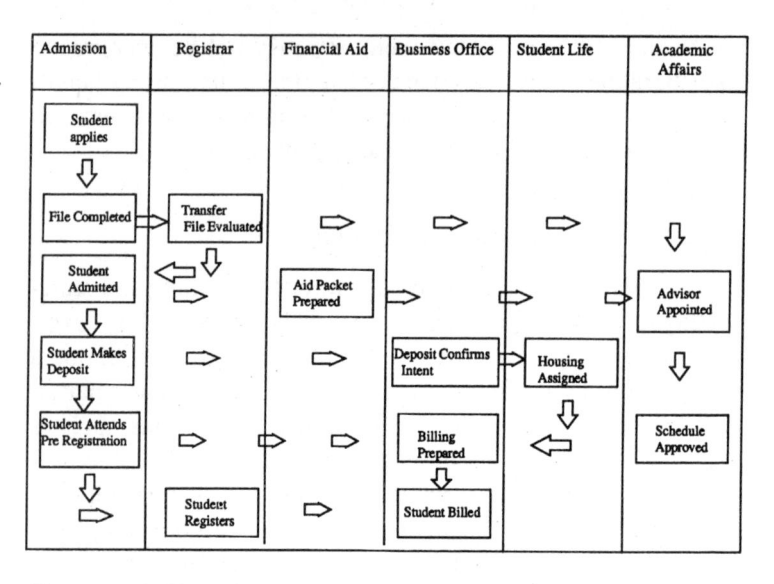

Admission	Registrar	Financial Aid	Business Office	Student Life	Academic Affairs
Student applies ⇩ File Completed ⇩ Student Admitted ⇩ Student Makes Deposit ⇩ Student Attends Pre Registration ⇩ ⇨	Transfer File Evaluated ⇩ ⇦ ⇨ ⇨ ⇨ Student Registers	⇨ Aid Packet Prepared ⇨ ⇨ ⇨	⇨ ⇨ Deposit Confirms Intent Billing Prepared ⇩ Student Billed	⇨ ⇨ Housing Assigned ⇩ ⇦	⇩ Advisor Appointed ⇩ Schedule Approved

Figure 4.2. Transfer student enrollment in a college.

This environment is sometimes hostile to cross-functional teams, though development teams for specific projects are highly energized. Team sponsorship is the most important factor in bringing team results to fruition.

Mapping

The flow chart is one of the most valuable tools for the cross-functional team. The team should map the process or processes affected by its project. Creating flow charts will allow the team to visualize the process across department and functional boundaries. One chart should cover major points. Members with expertise in each area can provide detail as the team advances. A simple chart of the process enrolling a transfer student in a college shows the number of departments involved (see Figure 4.2).

According to Carol Reichenberger, Vice President of Enrollment Management at Marian College, the process actually has more than 18 steps, each of which can be separately charted. Each requires some coordination across department lines.

The chart helps the team focus on processes rather than individuals and may reveal additional areas affected by the team's work. Since the team may discover that it requires additional information, communication, or even team members, the map should be created during planning. Though organizations with sophisticated chartering sometimes provide a process map employed in preliminary planning, the team should create its own to ensure understanding.

MEETING

The meeting is the cross-functional team's primary means of communication. Though e-mail and intranet services can be used to exchange information and track progress, they are by no means substitutes for face-to-face meetings, especially at early stages of a team project.

As important as they are, meetings can be a serious pitfall for teams. In the United States, the most important factor in work satisfaction is not pay or benefits, but "interesting work." There should be nothing more interesting than working toward a common goal with a diverse group of colleagues. However, the team meeting, like other meetings in the organization, often is seen as a burden, a time-waster.

It is important to set time limits for meetings and stick to them. Don't waste anyone's time. If resource people aren't needed at a meeting, don't require they attend. The leader should provide a purpose statement for every meeting.

There can be a disruptive, though passive, influence of non-participants at the meeting table. Those who "sit through" meetings without participating often complain that meetings lack purpose and they "tune out." A purpose statement should be a "one-liner" that keeps focus for the team. The purpose statement should include an explicit reference to the type of meeting being called. What is important is that each type of meeting requires a different form of participation and preparation. If persons know the type of meeting being called, they will also know what needs to be done in preparation for the meeting.

A meeting for decision-making requires preparation and structure. When problems are to be solved, there is an orientation toward the past at the outset. Data and records are important. Planning meetings have a future orientation and put emphasis on both creativity and project management. Status review meetings include discussion of problems, decisions, and plans. They are critical in advancing the project and assessing work. Specifying the type of meeting enables the team to prepare effectively and understand the flow of work in a managed project.

As the team explores the path of its project, it should note the kinds of meetings likely to be required. For example, as it reviews a communication plan, the team should schedule status review meetings with their sponsor and/or the chartering body. Since these meetings will require progress reports of the milestones reached and ongoing issues raised, they require more attention than ordinary sessions, especially since they call upon the team's presentation skills. Predicting the functions of meetings assists the team in seeing the "big picture" as their work unfolds and provides an understanding of their progress.

Individual meetings should also be evaluated for effectiveness. A simple checklist like the one below helps participants develop habits that support good meetings and encourage commitment to team processes. The checklist can be used for a quick review at the end of each meeting. New teams in particular benefit from tracking their performance from meeting to meeting.

SAMPLE MEETING CHECKLIST

LEADERSHIP
Did the meeting leader schedule the meeting and establish agenda?

AGENDA
Was there a clear, timed agenda? Were the purpose of the meeting and meeting type included?

MINUTES
Was a scribe appointed?
Were minutes distributed in a timely manner?

TIME
Was a timekeeper appointed?
Were time lines (start, stop, timed items) observed?

TEAMWORK
Did everyone attend?
Did everyone participate?
Were team guidelines for mutual respect followed?
Were decisions reached by consensus?
Was a clear process of decision-making followed?
Were positive achievements and trends, as well as problems, discussed?

FOCUS AND FOLLOW-UP
Did the meeting focus on issues important to associates?
Were results of the meeting translated to action?
Was there follow-up on decisions made at the last meeting?
Was everyone accountable for assignments delegated?
Was the meeting evaluated?

COLLABORATION AND COMMUNICATION
Were customers and appropriate members of management consulted/ involved, informed of issues and actions?

DECIDING

Consensus

The term "consensus" is probably familiar to most team members. In its strictest sense, it means total agreement, and has been identified as a pitfall for teams. Teams try so hard to agree that they don't benefit from constructive conflict, are unable to decide, and never get their job done.

However, in its best sense, consensus means that all members of the team agree that their viewpoints have had a fair hearing, that they accept the group's decision as the best alternative, and will support it. Consensus does not imply stifling dissent, rather the opposite. True consensus is only possible when all sides have been heard. In order to ensure that valuing consensus does not lead to indecision or grudging compliance, some teams establish a ground rule that if a member feels uneasy about a decision, he or she is allowed a day or two to advance reasoned objections that the group can explore. In the absence of reasoned objections, the decision goes forward. Another method teams employ to gain support for decisions is examining contingencies, sometimes using a Process Decision Program Chart (PDPC), a quality tool that maps what can go wrong in the implementation of a decision. In employing this tool, all members are able to decide on contingencies in the event of failure.

It's very important for team members to express disagreement or lack of understanding. This requires courage. Patience is also required by members listening to the disagreements or lack of understanding of others. These "virtues" pay off. During a team evaluation in a hospital, a member asserted that the team hadn't generated synergy with the rest of the organization. While several members ignored the evaluation, one persisted in getting a clear definition of what was meant. The result was a creative organizational "search conference" sponsored by the team. Results from the conference helped the team better communicate its strategic importance. Effective teams, however, should not have to rely only on persistent individuals.

Ground rules for establishing consensus build trust. If group members are ignored, or their ideas killed, little trust will result. Likewise, decisions initiated and supported by a few, or even a majority by vote, may find few supporters if they prove controversial. The team should therefore ensure that all voices are heard with respect and that voting not replace careful decision-making. In addition, a standard pattern for decision-making should be adopted.

Standardized Problem-Solving

Organizations identified as having the best practices for learning and improving have put in place standard problem-solving processes. These are given different names and may vary in the number of steps they go through. However, most follow the pattern of the process adopted and taught by Xerox Corporation. Systematic problem-solving provides clear expectations of how issues in planning, carrying out plans, and measuring results will be addressed. Over time, employees develop skills in analyzing processes rather than placing blame and in objectively testing out their ideas with others rather than "owning" solutions.

Standardized problem-solving (see Table 4.1) provides ways to handle conflict about facts and interpretations (cognitive conflict). It also reduces conflict based upon feelings (affective conflict). In the Xerox model, the team first identifies and selects a problem. The problem is analyzed and potential solutions are generated by its team. A solution is selected and a plan developed. The solution is then implemented and results are evaluated. A variety of "quality tools" are available for

Table 4.1. Problem-Solving Process

Problem-Solving Step	Question	The Cross-Functional Team
Identify and Select Problem	Where do we need change?	Should agree that a problem exists and describe how the organization should be after change. Don't assume that a problem is the same for everyone. State a specific goal to keep the team on track.
Analyze	Where are we now?	Study the present state. Use as many sources as available. Keep in mind that not everyone approaches a problem in the same way. Some prefer abstract concepts. Others prefer "hands on." Take advantage of different analytic skills on the team.
Generate Potential Solutions	Which idea has best potential?	Think outside the box. Don't limit solutions according to what functional departments can "buy."
Select and Plan Solution	What is the best action to take?	Don't blur differences. Strive for consensus but don't avoid reasoned objections. Use tools to create contingency plans.
Implement Solution	Do we have a plan?	Employ project management skills to define implementation. Keep lines of communication with stakeholders open. Communicate: **WHAT** is to be done. ACTION. **WHY** it will be done. STRATEGIC PERSPECTIVE. **HOW** it will be done. METHOD. TACTICAL PERSPECTIVE. **WHEN** it will be done. TIME LINE. **WHO** is responsible. RESPONSIBILITY. **MEASURE**. How do we know we've succeeded?
Evaluate	Did it work?	Apply agreed upon measures. Celebrate achievements.

teams to employ at each stage of problem-solving. Cross-functional teams especially need a wide range of decision-making tools to use flexibly in their deliberations.

A standard problem-solving process is important in providing teams with basic competence and confidence. Arriving at solutions is not always neat and mechanical, however. Often adaptability and flexibility are required, and the team may find that the problem presented to it needs to be reframed. Rarely do teams have a clear statement or definition of the problem before they begin working on it. Rather, such a statement often emerges only with difficulty over time and as a direct result of working on the problem. Cross-functional teams offer an advantage in defining and solving difficult problems because they include diverse perspectives and the opportunity for creativity. But they also need additional skills to succeed.

Author Nancy Dixon has identified some of these skills.

Skills for Team Dialogue

- Provide others accurate and complete information that is relevant to the issue.
- Assure others of their personal competence when disagreeing with their ideas.
- Make the reasoning that supports a position explicit; explain how the data led to the conclusion.
- Voice the perspective of others.
- Change your position when convincing data and rationale are offered.
- Regard assertions as hypotheses to be tested.
- Challenge errors in others' reasoning or data.

    Source: Nancy Dixon, *The Organizational Learning Cycle,* McGraw Hill, Inc., 1994. *Used with permission of the author.*

MANAGING CONFLICT

When asked what they fear about getting involved in team work, many members cite conflict, which is usually seen as negative in the workplace. While this response is legitimate, it applies to only one kind of conflict. Another, healthier sort is encouraged by good teams.

There are a number of sources for conflict:

- Differing goals
- Differing means to goals
- Scarce resources (money, power, time, etc.)
- Threats to identity

Effective definition of team goals, an effective project management and decision-making system, as well as clear allocation of resources contribute to reducing team conflict. However, in cross-functional teams there is an inherent threat to identity. One means by which individuals influence others is *expert power;* that is, they are respected for what they know. In attempting to create an egalitarian environment, cross-functional teams sometimes threaten subject matter experts. With everything open to question, experts may become defensive. Table 4.2 shows the challenge experts may face as they become cross-functional team members.

The emotions connected with expert power should not be underestimated. Even though a member may have been selected to participate in a team because of knowledge, interpretations based upon that expert knowledge may at times be discounted. The team member may get angry, and if not careful may appear arrogant. This experience may help members discover the degree to which they've relied on expert power in other facets of their work life. It is an opportunity to test interpersonal skills: in particular, accepting feedback nondefensively, remaining calm under stress, and checking understanding of others' ideas and values. One advantage of cross-functional teams that members should realize and employ to advantage is that we are generally less competitive with persons whose fields are different from our own. If one is in human resources, for example, it is probably less difficult for him or her to express admiration for the achievements of an engineer than of another human resource manager.

It is therefore important for cross-functional teams to establish a supportive environment for all members. In discussing ground rules, teams should consider the roles of experts as teachers, who clarify the logic of their disciplines for others. Questions therefore become learning opportunities, and all of those involved "own" the outcome of decision-making.

Table 4.2. Cross-Functional Team Perspective Shift

Functional Model	**Cross-Functional Team**
I work within my department or discipline	I identify with the goals of the team
I am an expert	I am a resource and a teacher
I define issues or problems in ways that lead to solutions that are preferred by my discipline or department	I define the issue or problem in ways that open paths to new solutions, perhaps by questioning departmental or discipline viewpoints
I maintain equilibrium and keep concerns to myself	I share concerns and needs for mutual understanding and resolution
I represent alternatives preferred by my department or discipline	I actively discuss and generate many alternatives
I stay within the rules of my department or discipline	I use decision-making tools that encourage multiple viewpoints, but lead to consensus

Conflict is also reduced by avoiding defensive communication. This is done by applying the qualities that create support for team members:

- Skills in describing a situation rather than judging or evaluating.
- A problem orientation rather than a control orientation.
- The ability to be spontaneous rather than being manipulated by a conscious strategy.
- Empathy rather than neutrality, where people retreat from their own identity into formal roles.
- Equality versus superiority.
- Provisionalism, seeking for answers, versus certainty.

The defenses are especially important to overcome in giving feedback to the team and to individual members. Barry Heermann calls this feedback "Letting Go." This means letting go of those things that keep us from attaining the service we are to perform. In giving feedback, it is important to remember that the main issue is team performance, not personalities.

The clearer the team makes its performance expectations, the easier it is for the leader or members to provide feedback on a team or individual basis. Feedback should be frequent for the team as a whole, so it's important to establish regular meeting and progress evaluations. Feedback should respect the persons to whom it is directed: it should be about things that can be changed. It should be specific, and it shouldn't be overwhelming. Failed teams sometimes "have it out" at the end of their work, regretting they hadn't spoken sooner and vowing never to serve on a team again. The emotions generated by such experiences cloud effective decision-making and organizational learning, which depends upon being able to interpret data together while appreciating a variety of perspectives.

CELEBRATING TEAM ACCOMPLISHMENTS

Attitudes toward reward and recognition reflect values. For many of us rewards are seen as individual. Others see them as creating "political" problems and division among work groups. Some see them as necessary motivators for peak performance. Reward and recognition are sensitive. Some organizations have shifted to programs that reward teams. These can be difficult to administer because a balance of individual and group performance is important to teams. Some include team skills and performance in evaluating individuals. They also include work on teams as part of employee workload and allocate personnel resources directly to the support of cross-functional teams.

In many instances, recognition may be more important than reward. Team leaders and members need to feel that their achievements are recognized as a contribution to the organization. Work on cross-functional teams should be included in any existing recognition system, and sponsors should be aware that ceremonial appreciation is significant, especially at the end of a team's life.

Throughout the life of successful teams, leaders and members openly express appreciation for contributions by individuals, and they create opportunities for affirmation of the team as a whole. These are sometimes social occasions, sometimes feedback on a milestone reached, sometimes the opportunity to speak in turn what members appreciate about one another. For some this may be uncomfortable; however, accepting positive feedback nonapologetically is an important skill in building spirit. With small rituals, teamwork is enhanced. At one manufacturing company, overall team effectiveness was enhanced when the president began to require that each member of the administrative team and quality council representatives report on team achievements at each meeting. The CEO of a medium-sized company initiated a dinner in honor of those participating in a new team initiative. All employees were invited, and the achievements of each team were proudly displayed.

Ritual is especially important when a team is disbanding. If the team experience has been good, members may expect to feel a little depression along with their success. If the team has attained high performance, the relationships established and creative energy generated will make concluding difficult. Members often feel regret as they abandon their roles and finish tasks. They should be permitted to share their experiences and should be acknowledged as their work ends.

CHAPTER 5
The Role of the Steering Team

Because cross-functional teams need resources and commitment from across the organization, they require legitimate authority. This usually comes from a quality council or steering committee. Where this body has not been established, or has no power—as in teams that cross business units—authority should come from the top management team.

The cross-functional team is usually established by a management team, quality council, or steering committee. This body has identified something that can best be addressed by looking across the organization: a problem for solution, a process for improvement or restructuring, a system for installation, a standard for certification (ISO 9000, QS-9000), an assessment for overall performance improvement (Baldrige), or a new product or service for development.

The role of those initiating a team cannot be overestimated. To charter a team for a mission that is not meaningful, is not supported, or is without result, is simply a waste of corporate resources and bad management.

The clearer the purposes, understanding, and commitment of the chartering body, the better the chances for team success. Since the bottom line measure for team success is meeting requirements established by the chartering body, those commissioning a cross-functional team should:

- Define and document the strategic importance of the team's project.
- Provide support for teams throughout the organization, including training.
- Understand how the team mission aligns with customers, suppliers, and core processes.
- Provide a clear mission for the team, including its scope and expected outcomes.
- Provide adequate resources to the team.
- Define sponsorship for the team.
- Define communication and feedback loops.

An organization new to quality initiatives may find considerable difficulty in addressing these points because it has not yet laid a groundwork for understanding its quality values and commitments, identifying customer needs, or mapping core processes. Without this groundwork, it will find problems in deploying cross-functional teams.

PURPOSE OF THE STEERING COMMITTEE

- Identify customer requirements and expectations.
- Communicate and operationalize these into the organization.
- Develop the quality vision for the organization.
- Develop quality policies.
- Identify quality goals for the organization.
- Identify critical quality objectives.
- Establish continuous improvement committees throughout the organization.
- Identify organizational requirements to achieve quality objectives.
- Approve and authorize resources.
- Monitor progress.
- Eliminate organizational road blocks.
- Take actions on problems or disputes.
- Coach and counsel senior managers on quality.

Source: Greg Hutchins, *The Quality Book, Quality Plus Engineering,* Portland, OR, 1996.

If an organization is beginning to employ cross-functional teams without a steering committee or similar body, it should consider establishing one to lay a quality foundation.

THE TEAM AND STRATEGY

Not all cross-functional teams are created equal. Some have greater strategic significance than others. However, as a general rule, because it spans functions, this type of team is likely to affect areas important to strategy. In each instance, therefore, the management team or steering committee needs to be aware of, and articulate how, formation of the team relates to corporate values and strategy. In an organization experienced in quality improvement, a problem-solving team may be quickly established and easily related to a corporate value of continuous improvement. But, on the other hand, a team assigned to develop a new product or service may be the result of long and sophisticated market analysis and planning. It may also represent a change in corporate direction.

Answering some key questions will assist the chartering body in assessing and communicating the strategic importance of a team.

- What corporate values does the team embody?
- Is the team's mission aligned with our communicated strategy?
- How will our organization be different if the team completes its work?
- Which processes and systems will be affected?
- Which customers (internal and external) will be most affected?
- Which suppliers will be most affected?
- How will the "bottom line" (financial results) be improved?

- How will we be better able to change and grow in the future?
- How will our organizational identity be affected?

In answering these questions, three factors should be kept in mind: the importance of any change being considered, present performance in the area, and opportunity for improvement. Explicit measures of performance should be identified.

This approach also provides discipline in forming teams. It enhances process and customer focus while helping to define who may be involved in the team and what outcomes are to be expected.

In organizations where cross-functional teams are new, or have had significant problems, the chartering body should also review some of its assumptions about management, values, and empowerment practices.

- Management

    Have we aligned our employee team participation system with strategic objectives?

    Have we instilled management responsibility for quality?

    Do our managers value interdependence?

    Do our managers have sponsorship skills to support team projects to completion?

- Shared Values

    Do we have a system for making our values explicit?

    Are we ready to change?

    Are we free to challenge assumptions?

    How do we handle diversity?

    Do we need to include new and diverse perspectives from stakeholders?

- Empowerment
    Have teams been confined to issues of daily process control?
    Are employee decision-making skills fully developed?
    Is a climate of participation fostered?
    Are solutions limited by what the boss might think?

SUPPORT AND TRAINING

Some organizations may find they need to enhance team training. Others may need to create an environment friendly to cross-functional teams. For example, a publishing company began at the top, with the leader communicating his intention to initiate strategic change through teams.

A professionally facilitated workshop for top managers defined a vision of teamwork based upon core division values, critical success factors for realizing the vision, and a managerial commitment to action in providing structured communication channels and a decision-making process.

Middle managers received top management's commitments in a similar workshop, and provided feedback on what they would need to implement new roles in a team environment. Finally, line employees provided specific requests for the support they would need to participate in the new model. A corporate team handbook became a chartering document, a record of a process of collaborative decision-making and of commitment to role model behavior to foster teamwork. New corporate norms were created and affirmed across the organization. The following list shows the process that was employed in this example.

SHIFT TO A TEAM ENVIRONMENT

1. Senior management commitment to teamwork: Senior management defines drivers for organizational success. Makes personal/corporate commitment to behavioral/process change through statement of role model leadership. Translates into strategies. Communicates strategy and underlying model to middle-managers.

2. Line managers commit to a behavioral model based upon strategy.

3. Behavioral model and level of senior management support communicated to employees, who provide feedback on what they require to implement.

4. On the job, systematic support for new behaviors provided. Employees, line managers, senior managers assess progress in reaching strategic objectives. As teams are formed, their work is supported, measured, assessed, and recognized.

Where team training is required, the initial focus should be on customer orientation, process mapping, and problem-solving. Though team skills are learned by individuals, training should be integrated with immediate practice, usually at first within departments or functions. No training should be undertaken until the corporation integrates teamwork into its overall strategy and defines uniform systems for its deployment.

Generally, team training includes:

- Orientation to customers and stakeholders.
- Exercises that demonstrate that teams work: the greater effectiveness of group decisions.

- Interpersonal dynamics: stages of small group development.
- Team roles and goals: team leader and member roles. Writing an effective mission statement.
- A structured decision-making process.
- Process awareness and mapping.
- Use of quality tools: seven quality-control tools, seven management and planning tools, and increasingly, tools for creativity, including varieties of brainstorming, and project management techniques.

CUSTOMER, SUPPLIER, AND CORE PROCESS ALIGNMENT

Organizations exist to serve their customers. Those chartering a cross-functional team should assess the impact of the team's project on the organization's customers, suppliers, and processes. Customers are those who benefit from our work, and include final customers, who receive services or products, intermediate customers, such as distributors, and internal customers, such as departments or employees receiving output from one another. Suppliers, whether internal or external, provide input—product, service, or sometimes information. "Customer driven" organizations focus on customer satisfaction, providing not only expected or desired quality, but exceeding customer expectations with "excited quality." Processes transform and add value to inputs; for example, in a manufacturing process, raw materials are transformed into a product, or in a consultation, financial or human resource data become a report or plan. In traditional corporations, processes frequently cross departmental or functional boundaries, and though we hear of "process owners" (those who have oversight and authority over a process), true owners are sometimes hard to find. While this situation offers real opportunity for process improvement using cross-functional teams, it also creates "political" issues that the teams themselves cannot resolve. Therefore, it is important for the chartering body to identify the core process(es) and "owners" affected by the team project, along with customer and supplier issues.

Identifying customers, suppliers, and processes enables the chartering body to see at a macro-level the possible impact of the team, more effectively assess required resources, and choose a leader with the skills required to interface with a variety of departments or functions.

Once the team itself begins work, it will have to explore processes and interfaces in greater detail. In fact, part of the team's work is often discovery, especially if its task is process improvement. The team may find that processes go awry when they cross functional boundaries. It will be the team's job to help the organization learn about the process as it decides on corrective action. Another important consideration for both the chartering body and the team is identification of stakeholders. For our purposes, stakeholders may be defined as persons or organizations not directly involved in the customer-supplier chain or process under examination, but whose interests may be affected. At times, as in an installation of an ISO 9000 quality system, a large number of stakeholders may be affected. Or, in the case of new product development, corporate image, tradition and customer product loyalty may be at stake—as in the introduction of "New Coke."

Cross-functional teams must be sensitive to their range of stakeholders, and communication about their project has to be carefully managed from the time of chartering.

DEFINING PURPOSE: TEAM MISSION

The team's mission, what it is expected to accomplish, should be clearly defined. The team is chartered because someone (whether a manager, council member, employee, customer, or supplier) has identified a gap in performance or service, or the corporation has set a new strategy. Whether addressing a performance gap or creating a new product or service, the cross-functional team should be provided with a description of the present situation and a "desired state." The desired state describes how the process, product, organization, or personnel will be different when the team has completed its work. In describing the present situation, it's often helpful to the team to have some history of the problem or opportunity to be addressed. In defining the desired state, expected measures of success are also helpful. For example, the distribution manager at a newspaper in a small city notes that sales at kiosks are 24% lower when the paper arrives at the point of sale after 11:00 am. He has observed that late deliveries are usually caused by late production. He calculates that late delivery is costing more than $40,000 per year. The management group charters a cross-functional team to improve delivery time. The future state is simply defined: Papers are delivered to kiosks by 11:00 am. The team may face a formidable task in improving production deadlines, but it has a clear purpose and knows the benefits of success.

TEAM RESOURCES

Resources available to the team should be specified and budgeted. As closely as possible, the chartering body should estimate the duration and cost of the team's project. For the most part, costs are incurred in people. It is important to provide time for the team leader to conduct team business. In turn, the team leader should be able to negotiate for the time of team members. Other costs may be identified in equipment and materials, or consulting services. Personnel costs are especially significant for cross-functional teams. Leaders and members will spend their time working outside of their own functions. Part of the reluctance employees sometimes feel about joining cross-functional teams is related to demands on their time, combined with stress placed upon them by their managers, whose departmental resources are being stretched. The team charter should include an estimate of resource costs for the team to complete its project. Budget control should also be considered, with the possibility for the team to negotiate for budget changes as it more clearly defines its work activities.

SPONSORSHIP

The sponsor of a cross-functional team should be that manager or council member who has the most significant strategic buy-in to the team's mission. That is, the person who has the greatest interest in making the organization different through the team's project. The sponsor provides power, time, energy and resources to the team. Power simply means legitimate authority to get things done, as well as the ability to influence areas outside of one's direct control. The sponsor should maintain regular communication with the team leader and support the leader's efforts in obtaining cooperation across the organization. Since cross-functional teams not only require members from different departments, who might be missed by their bosses, but also information and expertise from many sources, the sponsor's support is critical.

COMMUNICATION

The chartering body should establish a communication plan to support the use of cross-functional teams throughout the organization and to contribute to the success of individual teams. Without communication, cross-functional teams can themselves become "silos," running in parallel and not across the organization.

The sponsoring body should answer key questions on its communications strategy:

- ♦ Do we communicate effectively among ourselves?
  - Role model teamwork begins here. Without regular interaction, the steering team cannot reach high performance. Without regular monitoring and interpretation of data on team performance by the council, little or no positive change will take place over time. Interpretation as well as information is required for full functioning.

- ♦ Do we clearly communicate strategic objectives and change? Is our practice consistent and timely? Do we give the appearance of working in secret?
  - Vision needs to be shared.
  - Participation, team development, and trust are closely related.
  - Fear impedes a change process and reduces positive motivation.

- ♦ Do we carefully design our communications?
  - Messages are likely to be misinterpreted. They should be clear.

- Communication should be designed to reinforce core values and role model behaviors. "Preaching" isn't necessary. Meaningful interpretation of work is.

♦ Do we use multiple communication channels?
- Choose the medium of communication carefully. Don't defer to technology just because it's simpler to e-mail. The grapevine is so powerful because it relies on face-to-face encounters.
- Employ redundancy. Messages need to be repeated, and usually a number of media are more effective than one.

♦ Have "feedback loops" been established with cross-functional teams and those their work affects?
- When employees have unanswered questions, the grapevine (which exists in every organization) takes over and supplies answers. These "answers" are sometimes linked to employee fears and paint a negative picture. The steering team needs to see the effects of their own messages: Listen.
- The steering team needs to take account of reactions by stakeholders and process owners. They can assist cross-functional teams with effective communication, feedback, attitude change. They can also sabotage teams. The steering team needs to review the cross-functional team's plan for communication.
- Feedback of evaluation, including appropriate recognition, will keep team objectives on track. Without interpretation and evaluation of what's happening on all levels, the team initiative will fade.

CREATING THE FUTURE: ALIGNING FOR RESULTS

Some organizations exploring "the basics of cross-functional teams" may feel it impractical to apply the criteria of the Malcolm Baldrige National Quality Award, established to support performance excellence in United States companies. However, reviewing how the organization deploys cross-functional teams can provide a simple internal assessment of both an organization's values and its orientation to Baldrige criteria (see Table 5.1).

Table 5.1. Baldrige Categories/Corporate Values

Baldrige Categories	Corporate Values	Team Deployment Action
1. *Leadership.* Involvement of leadership in creating and sustaining quality values and deploying them through systems.	*Collaboration.* The ability of leadership to co-operate independently with all levels of management to insure attainment of quality goals.	Quality Council or similar body charters teams. Sponsorship and resources clearly defined.
2. *Strategic Planning.* Creation of strategy and action plans that connect with performance management.	*Mission.* The ability of a corporation to establish goals and execute plans that take into account how the company meets the needs of customers and society.	Teams are chartered in line with strategic objectives. Strategy becomes a set of criteria for chartering teams.
3. *Customer and Market Focus.* Determination of customer and market expectations and requirements. Customer relationship enhancement and determination of satisfaction.	*Human Dignity.* Consciousness of the right of every person to have his or her needs met and to grow. "Quality is the totality of features and characteristics of a product or service that bears on its ability to satisfy a given need."— ISO-8402	Customers, stakeholders, and suppliers affected by the team project are identified and their needs assessed.
4. *Information and Analysis.* Information management for effective process and performance management systems.	*Criteria and Rationality.* Fact-based decision-making. Trained capacity to make decisions from data. *Communication of Information.* Effective transmission of ideas and information throughout the organization.	Information systems support teams. Communication loops are established. Clear processes for fact-based decision-making and conflict resolution are established.
5. *Human Resource Development and Management.* Alignment of employee growth and corporate purpose. Creation of a quality human environment.	*Self-Competence and Confidence.* Realistic and objective confidence that one has the skills to achieve in a quality organization and to feel that those skills are a positive contribution.	Team skills are enhanced. Leadership skills are deployed throughout the organization and team accomplishments are recognized.
6. *Process Management.* Effective customer-focused design, management, and improvement of processes. Supplier partnering.	*Evaluation of Self and System.* Appreciating self-evaluation and making application of objective standards to the operation of systems.	The team evaluates itself and improves systems. It focuses on processes that cross functional boundaries.
7. *Business Results.* Key performance measures in customer satisfaction, finance and market, human resources, supplier and partner performance, and operations.	*Achievement and Success.* Accomplishing noteworthy, measurable results through focus on outcomes.	Team results are measured. Lessons learned are captured.

CHAPTER 6
Conclusion

Cross-functional teams are a way of working together that signals a shift in organizational thinking, a shift toward process and project, and away from function and department. They provide a way of deploying strategic initiatives and developing leadership skills throughout the workforce. Though they gained prominence in manufacturing companies, they are equally useful to education and other non-profits, as well as the broad range of service industries and organizations. Wherever they are employed, they require some "basics:"

- Management commitment to aligning teams with corporate objectives.

- An effective system for establishing corporate direction and resources for teams.

- Careful selection of team projects and personnel.

- A systems perspective not only for management, but for the team.

- Understanding of corporate and team values.

- Development of team skills in project planning, including measuring results.
- Development of interpersonal skills supported by a formal decision-making process.
- Communication loops to keep teams aligned with the organization.
- Ongoing focus on outcomes, supported by celebration of accomplishments.
- Commitment by the organization, team leaders, and members to evaluate the work of teams.

These go beyond quality tools and understanding of internal team dynamics, they demand integration of organizational thinking about quality. Individual cross-functional teams can, and do, enjoy success in improvement projects. Though these are worthwhile, if the organization has not attended to "basics," it may soon find such projects isolated and readily abandoned with shifts in strategy.

However, with foundations in place, cross-functional teams can help transform an organization, deploying quality values, contributing to business results, and building competence throughout the organization.

References

Dixon, N. (1994). *The Organizational Learning Cycle.* New York: McGraw Hill.

Employers' Needs Working Council (1992). *A Report of the Total Quality Leadership Steering Committee and Working Councils* (Total Quality Forum). Cincinnati: Procter and Gamble.

Hall, B. and Rosen, L. (1995). *Values-Based Teaching Skills.* Rockport, MA: Twin Lights.

Hutchins, G. (1996). *The Quality Book.* Portland, OR: Quality Plus Engineering.

Mitroff, I.I. and Linstone, H.A. (1993). *The Unbounded Mind.* New York: Oxford University Press.

Renesch, J. and Defoore, B., eds. (1996). *The New Bottom Line, Bringing Heart and Soul to Business.* San Francisco: New Leader Press.

Yuckl, G. (1994). *Leadership in Organizations.* Englewood Cliffs, NJ: Prentice Hall.

Further Reading

Brown, Mark Graham, *Baldrige Award Winning Quality: How to Interpret the Malcolm Baldrige Award Criteria*, 7th ed. 1997.

———. *Keeping Score: Using the Right Metrics to Drive World-Class Performance*. 1996.

Damelio, Robert. *The Basics of Process Mapping*. 1996.

Dew, John R. *Quality-Centered Strategic Planning: A Step-by-Step Guide*. 1997.

DeWeaver, Mary Feeherry, and Gillespie, Lori Ciprian. *Real-World Project Management: New Approaches for Adapting to Change and Uncertainty*. 1997.

Harbour, Jerry L., Ph.D. *The Basics of Performance Measurement*. 1997.

Parry, Scott B. *From Managing to Empowering: An Action Guide to Developing Winning Facilitation Skills*. 1994.

Pike, Wilbur L. III. *Leading the Transition: Management's Role in Creating a Team-Based Culture.* 1995.

Rabbitt, John T. and Bergh, Peter A. *The ISO 9000 Book: A Global Competitor's Guide to Compliance and Certification,* 2nd ed. 1994.

———. *The QS-9000 Miniguide.* 1997.

Please contact Quality Resources at 1-800-247-8519 for information on the above books.

Other QR publications in the "Basics" series

The Basics of Benchmarking
Robert Damelio
74 pp., 1995, Item No. 763012, paperback

The Basics of Performance Measurement
Jerry L. Harbour, Ph.D.
71 pp., 1997, Item No. 763284, paperback

The Basics of Process Mapping
Robert Damelio
65 pp., 1996, Item No. 763160, paperback

The Basics of FMEA
Robin E. McDermott, Raymond J. Mikulak, and Michael R. Beauregard
76 pp., 1996, Item No. 763209, paperback

The Basics of Mistake-Proofing
Robin E. McDermott, Raymond J. Mikulak, and Micharl R. Beauregard
66 pp., 1997, Item No. 763276, paperback

The Basics of Idea Generation
Donna Greiner
64 pp., 1977, Item No. 76339X, paperback

For additional information on any of the above titles, or to request a catalog, call 800-247-8519.

Quality Resources, 902 Broadway, New York, NY 10010